Cutting Through the

BS

For the **LOVE**
of Network Marketing

THOMAS DUBOIS

Cutting Through the BS, for the LOVE of Network Marketing
Published by LTJ, inc.
Aspen, Colorado

ISBN: 978-1-7365368-0-3
BUSINESS & ECONOMICS / Marketing / Multilevel

Cover and Interior design by Victoria Wolf,
wolfdesignandmarketing.com

QUANTITY PURCHASES: companies, professional groups, clubs, and other organizations may qualify for special terms when ordering quantities of this title. For information, email thomas@ cuttingthroughthebs.com.

*This book is dedicated to my beautiful wife
Laura for trusting in the person I have become, more
than the person I was! She is my partner,
my best friend, and my everything!*

*To my daughter Jaedium, son-in-law Dante,
and grandchildren Noah & Lorelai!*

*My brother Bob Dubois for bailing me out in my
addiction days and believing in me enough to help
me get started on my Entrepreneurial journey!*

*To EVER SINGLE PERSON that every joined me in
business and teammates I have had for years, you
know who you are. When I say I love my team, the
words are not held lightly in my heart! Each one of
your successes has added to all of mine and there
is no way this book is possible without you!!*

Contents

Introduction 1

   The Summer of 2019 1

   Why Me? And Why This Book? 2

   My Story 4

   The Rest of My Story 7

   Why Networking Marketing? 8

   In This Book 13

   How This Book Is Organized 15

Chapter 1: Expose the *Wrong* Expectations 17

   Making Your "Why" *Alive* 17

   Outright Lies and Exaggerations about What to Expect 19

Chapter 2: Set the **Right** Expectations 31

   The Very First Expectation 32

   Set the Right Expectations with the Tommy T 33

Chapter 3: The Steps to Success in Network Marketing 45

   Starting the Conversation 46

Become a Professional Inviter 54

Do I Really Need to Pitch to My Friends? 61

You've Got Them Interested. Now What?
The Value of the Third Party 62

The Key to Success 63

Chapter 4: The Tools to Succeed in
Network Marketing 79

Two Hundred Marbles 79

Easy-Peasy 80

The Direct Contact Easy-Peasy System 81

The Power of Intention 84

Tough Times 88

Affirmations 89

The Tens 93

The Ten Questions 94

The Ten Biggest Mistakes People Make When
Joining a Network Marketing Company 96

Supporting Your Team 99

Share This Book, Share These Steps 100

Acknowledgments 103

About the author 105

Introduction

The Summer of 2019

In the summer of 2019, I hit one of the lowest points in my career: I found out that someone involved in the industry I love was, once again, creating the wrong expectations in people who sincerely wanted to succeed—people who, I felt, deserved better. I'd seen it before, but this time something inside me shifted. I wanted to set the record straight. I wanted to confront the wrong teaching and start shouting the right expectations from the rooftops.

Cutting through the BS: for the LOVE of Network Marketing is the result of that day. This book is about exposing the *wrong* expectations for network marketing. It is about setting the *right* expectations. And it is about the steps you can take to achieve success in this industry.

WHY ME? AND WHY THIS BOOK?

I'm Thomas Dubois, and I wrote *Cutting through the BS* because I got tired of seeing people hurt by people in the network marketing industry setting the wrong expectations and, therefore, setting people up for failure. I got tired of network marketing companies promising pie in the sky to people who actually needed assistance in setting the right expectations, the right mindset, and the right methods and practices, to produce real results so *anybody* could have success.

I also got tired of the opposite: people calling an industry that has delivered quality products and services to my family and friends for much of my adult life, and provided opportunities to many of them to make a living in the process, a *scam.* I got tired of hearing names like "pyramid scheme," "Ponzi scheme," "the NFL Club—the No Friends Left Club," "another one of *those* things," and all the other names used for an industry that I've made my life's work—an industry that changes lives for the better.

Of course, we all know what cutting through the BS means. But, how about an alternative meaning? How about, cutting through the *belief system* of network marketing? Just like anything else we do, we have to believe in what we are doing. We have to believe in what we are selling or teaching or the service we are providing. This belief system provides the support for whatever it is we do.

In this book I want to give you all I've got.

In this book I want to give you all I've got. I want to save you from making the mistakes I made and share with you the things I did right. I want you to be part of my team, even if it is virtual and the only place we meet is here, in the pages of this book.

On the other hand, I want you to know that you have infinite value for me because, first, you are receiving my words as well as my belief in you and my desire for your success. You might even become a valued member of my team and be part of growth and success that could provide you with prosperity beyond your wildest imaginings and, in turn, provide me with the same. In other words, network marketing is about value—recognizing and sharing value with others through building a successful business.

Are you with me?

MY STORY

Before we go much further, I need to tell you my story. Because if I can succeed at this business, starting at the bottom where I found myself, I believe you can too.

In 1999, I was attempting drug and alcohol rehabilitation through a program offered by a last chance rehab based in Houston, Texas. The program offered a last resort for addicts. It put me to work, as it put all its participants to work, because work is part of its rehabilitation program. The truth is, that's really the only part of its program. And this work is unpaid.

So, unpaid, I was shoveling cow and horse manure at the Houston Rodeo. Before that, I had been cleaning up the side of a highway. And, at the risk of punishment in the form of public humiliation of one kind or another, I challenged the staff on what I thought were abusive practices. Just so you know, challenging wasn't acceptable.

I got kicked out.

Homeless

Within hours, I was homeless, walking down the streets of Houston with my clothes, my only belongings, in two plastic trash bags.

I had nowhere to turn. My family had had enough, but my mom decided to relent and get me a motel room in Houston for the night. As I carried my bags to the motel, one began to rip. I put it down, deciding to come back for it. I got to the motel, put my one bag of clothes in the room, and went back to get the other bag. It was gone.

I was homeless, with one bag of clothes, and one night paid at a run-down motel. The next day, I found Texas House, another last-ditch, work-based drug and alcohol rehabilitation program, except that this program included twelve-step meetings. I stayed there for several months.

That was the beginning of my last, and my best, chance.

A Bit of Sobriety

Day after day, I worked, went to twelve-step meetings, and learned what it was like to live life without constantly turning to drugs or alcohol. In other words, I got a little bit of sobriety under my belt. Perhaps sensing the change, or maybe because he couldn't bring himself to allow me to miss it, my dad bought me a bus ticket to attend my little sister's wedding. And for the first time in my life, at that wedding, I felt it might be possible to actually live a life of sobriety. I knew I had to continue going to twelve-step meetings as if my life depended on it—because it did.

I went back to Texas House, continued with my program, and after what may have been months, came back to Denver, where I am from. I found new twelve-step meetings and a new community in Denver and, within a few years, I was introduced to my entrepreneurial career by my brother, Bob. Bob had bought a direct mail advertising franchise. He saw that I had achieved some sobriety and, for the umpteenth time, he took a chance on me and offered me the opportunity to run the business.

This was the first time I was introduced to sales, self-direction, and self-motivation. I thrived. It turned out that working as an entrepreneur was key to how I could succeed. Within two years, I turned one franchise into three.

Our Family's Angel

Then a good friend of ours, Erik Bakewell, along with his wife, Marcella, introduced Bob to network marketing. Bob, in turn, introduced me. As Bob and I learned a new industry, I saw Bob's success grow. Convinced in the possibility of success, I dove right in after him. Soon I was making six figures, and I made network marketing my only career. My dad ended up calling Erik "our family's angel."

Network marketing became my life.

THE REST OF MY STORY

By 2008, just six years into my network marketing career, my wife, Laura, and I had the opportunity to realize a dream. Laura had been a dog groomer for thirteen years. The idea of owning her own grooming shop had been with her for most of those years, but that dream seemed completely out of reach. She had worked at a shop in Boulder for ten of those years. She had recently asked for a raise, and her boss shook her head and said, "No. Just do more dogs."

Laura was in charge of going through the mail at the grooming salon, and one day a postcard arrived advertising the sale of a dog grooming shop located in Aspen, Colorado. Laura texted me. Half-joking, she asked, "You want to buy a dog grooming shop?"

Without hesitating, I texted, "Let's buy it."

Barking Beauties

Within three months, we were on our way to Glenwood Springs, Colorado, proud owners of Barking Beauties Dog Spa in nearby Aspen. Barking Beauties quickly became the place where elite dog owners of Aspen take their dogs to look good and smell good and grace their lovely mountain homes.

We love living and working surrounded by those beautiful mountains, aspen trees, and green meadows. In addition to owning Barking Beauties, we are proud owners of multiple businesses.

Over the last twenty years, I have taken those businesses to top levels. I have a passion for helping others in sobriety, and I am on the board of directors for four sober living homes in Parker, Colorado, called Step Seven Ministries.

We have a beautiful daughter, Jaedium, and son-in-law, Dante. We have been blessed by them with two beautiful grandchildren.

God, family, friends, and the thousands of people I have had the pleasure and honor to meet through network marketing are everything to me.

WHY NETWORKING MARKETING?

I love network marketing. By this time, you probably know why. But I'll say it anyway: I love network marketing because I love helping others achieve a livable income—or maybe even more—just like I did, by making products and services available to the people who can benefit from them most. I love giving people opportunity, just as I experienced opportunity, no matter where they are in their lives when they accept that opportunity. I love opening a world of community and teamwork, self-motivation, and the joy of directly benefitting from your own labors.

Network marketing *works.* Network marketing allows an individual to work on his or her own to create a successful business with no capital or an investment of just a few hundred dollars. That individual can join others and, together as a team, become a powerful force that changes lives.

Network marketing allows an individual to work on his or her own to create a successful business with no capital or an investment of just a few hundred dollars.

The Business Model

A traditional business model requires investment capital, staff, and entire departments of people. On the other hand, the multilevel marketing (also known by the acronym MLM) business model usually relies on just a few people providing back office support with the real work being done by an army of individuals providing the sales and marketing. Network marketing is the fastest, most inexpensive, way to bring a product to market and distribute it widely.

Network marketing is also called direct sales, direct marketing, relationship marketing, referral marketing. I'll be using those terms interchangeably. MLM can be done by itself or on off hours for someone who has a full-time job. In other words, network marketing can fit nearly anyone's schedule and nearly anyone's circumstances.

Everybody Is Equal

MLM can be done from home, by people with little or no experience or training, learning as they go. If it's a properly run company, everybody starts at the same place and has the same opportunity to get to the top. In contrast, corporate America reserves the top for only a chosen few.

If you want results, network marketing provides them. *Big* results. I have not had to work in a traditional business for sixteen years. I've seen hundreds of people do more than just make a living. I've seen them change their lives, educate themselves, and develop focus and positive thinking—skills that serve them not just in their business but in their entire lives.

Personal Growth with a Paycheck

Network marketing may be one of the most powerful methods of changing a life. In my organizations, we call it personal growth with a paycheck.

Most people come to network marketing because of dissatisfaction with the way their lives and careers have turned out. In fact, some people may arrive at network marketing because they have very few choices left. They have to make a change.

That's how I arrived: with very few choices and the need to make a change.

I Had to Get Sober

The change I needed to make, quite simply, was to get sober.

I suppose, though, that before even the desire to get sober took hold, there was something else: the desire for success. I had to face the fact that what I had been doing wasn't working. No matter how much of my time and energy I put into it—and believe me, I put a great deal of time and effort into my poor choices and the selfish pursuit of addiction— I was driving my life, my health, my relationships, and my finances right into the ground.

What if I could put even some of that time and effort into something useful—something that could make me money and erase some of the shame and loss I and those I loved had experienced?

I Discovered Network Marketing

In discovering network marketing, I discovered a path of entrepreneurial activity that could provide a man with a past with the experience of accomplishment and whatever he wanted. I learned I could make great money, consistently, in this industry that can give anyone, regardless of background, a real opportunity for financial freedom and personal success.

No Credibility

As a recovered addict, just three years into recovery when I began taking this industry seriously, *I had no credibility.* I'll talk about this in greater detail later in the book but, through third-party testimonials in the form of three-way phone calls, *I could use other people's credibility.*

I was a criminal without education, with a twenty-year history of drug addiction and a felony to boot, but through using other people's systems provided in network marketing, my credibility didn't matter. I was able to use other people's credibility until I had my own.

Network marketing is a place for second chances. For a few who see the opportunity immediately, it's a place for first chances. But most of us aren't that blessed. Either way, as a first chance or third chance or even a last chance, networking marketing works! Any background or any of these starts can turn into dreams fulfilled.

I love public speaking, and I loved writing this book because both of these forms of communication allow me to give away all the information I have accrued so *you* can be successful. I don't think you can truly keep network marketing success unless you give it away.

Your Takeaway

What I want somebody to walk away with after I give a talk, or have as a takeaway for you when you are done reading this book, is the belief that anybody can have success. I feel confident that no matter what their background, no matter what level of success they may have reached before, others can do what I have done.

I love what I do. And I get to do what I love! When you do what you love, it's not really work. I want you to give up working and start loving what you do.

Network marketing lets you do that. Network marketing lets you love what you do.

IN THIS BOOK

In this book, I am going to share my own experiences, both the hardships and the victories, through personal testimony. I won't be lying to you about how I built my business. I will not candy-coat, polish, or deny the truths of how I built my businesses.

The message I want you to come away with from this book is that, with the right training, setting the right expectations, and using the right tools, anyone can succeed with network marketing. Any background, even a collection of false starts like I had, can turn into dreams fulfilled.

With these words, I hope to pass on my success, so that I might keep it. That is the message of twelve-step programs, and that is a message I have learned to live by: **As we assist others by sharing our own experience of success, we solidify our own success**. Thank you for allowing me to do that in these pages.

This Information Comes from My Heart

I am sharing the information that I have gleaned through the years from *my* heart. I hope you will open *your* heart to receive it. I want you to have a chance to benefit, as I have, from an industry that rewards your efforts directly, and everyone shares the same equal opportunities from the day they start. To me, the corporate world is the *true* pyramid scheme: There's one person at the top who reaps the greatest benefits. As you go down the org chart, as you go down through varying levels in the structure of the company, the benefits decrease. That top person is benefitting from the work of those below him or her.

In contrast, direct marketing is *direct:* I connect *directly* with you so we both *directly* benefit. Your business is as big as you can make it, and so is mine.

I Love Network Marketing

It's really simple for me: I love network marketing because it brings to market some of the best products and services I have found—products and services that are innovative and effective, products and services that bring value to me and the people I share them with. My family would agree. And network marketing can produce some *serious* income. There is no need to exaggerate or falsify expectations because if I can do it, so can you.

If I can do it, so can you.

HOW THIS BOOK IS ORGANIZED

This book is organized into three chapters. These three chapters will help you:

- expose the BS that runs through the direct sales industry and avoid the wrong expectations

- implement the right expectations

- learn some simple tools and what it takes to succeed in network marketing

Let's go!

CHAPTER 1

EXPOSE THE *WRONG* EXPECTATIONS

MAKING YOUR "WHY" *ALIVE*

You need a big dream. In the industry, we call it a big, hairy, audacious goal. But that dream is *yours* and if I prospect you, I cannot promise you *your* dream. Again, that's yours. And as your sponsor, it's my job to break that dream down into smaller, realistic, *achievable* goals.

If someone is sharing an opportunity with you and they promise you will achieve your biggest dream, they are setting the wrong expectation.

I am sick and tired of people who should be experiencing success not doing so because they have been exposed to the wrong expectations. Some people quit three feet from gold, as the saying goes. They don't succeed because they quit.

I don't want that to be you.

Why Are There Wrong Expectations?

The number one reason someone might share wrong expectations is greed. The person in front of you, the person pitching a product or service to you, the person *pitching a business to you*—because that's really the most important aspect of the sale of a product or service brought to you through direct sales—if that person sets wrong expectations, it's to make a sale. This is damaging in two ways: If you give that person the sale, if you buy that person's product or service, you will likely be disappointed in the business you build. *But perhaps the bigger damage comes when you base your business practices on the same business practices that were used to recruit you and then you, in turn, set the wrong expectations to those you approach.*

Setting the wrong expectation is doing nothing but ruining this industry I love. And I want you to love this industry, too!

The Success of Top Leaders Is Not Likely to be the Immediate Success of New Team Members

In network marketing, some people, when presenting a new business, product or service to others, might claim that the successes of the top leaders are obtainable by someone who has just entered that business. This can easily ruin the expectations of someone who does not yet have the skill level of those top leaders. Through true *teachable* and *coachable* mentorship, people can reach success. But that success requires practice to increase skill level. Such success doesn't happen overnight, and it doesn't fit "get rich quick" expectations.

If the expectations that are shared with new team members are actually the results of top producers rather than of new team members, people will end up feeling like they were lied to. Instead, I believe realistic expectations, along with goal-setting and sharing tools and steps to success, are the way to go.

That's what this book is about.

OUTRIGHT LIES AND EXAGGERATIONS ABOUT WHAT TO EXPECT

Here are some of the wrong expectations shared when people are prospecting that I have heard all too often over my years in this business. Unfortunately, I'm sure, in time, I will hear more!

"You will soon be making six or seven figures."

Sure, but you may need to, first, pay the rent and achieve some smaller goals. You may need to supplement your income, reach a few moderate goals, and then move on to a livable income. *Then* decide you are ready to make a six-figure income your goal, all while you are dreaming *big*!

"You'll have hundreds of team members."

Again, sure, but let's start with who you want to have in your business. You might be working together for years, going to conventions or perhaps on a cruise, so you want them to be people you love and respect.

"If you just get two ..."

Some people will tell you, "You don't need one hundred people; you don't need fifty people. If you just get *two people,* and help *them* get two people, you'll be on your way."

It's true that it takes only two good people, but you will likely have to go through the numbers to find your two people. There isn't a network marketer I know who hasn't had to go through hundreds, if not thousands, of people to find two who will make them anywhere from a livable income to a six- or seven-figure income. The millionaires? They simply did whatever it took, and presented their product or service or program to as many people as they needed to, to get where they wanted to be.

"I need to convince my best friend or my former business partner to join my business."

The thinking is that if I can just get this person or that person, then I can grow my business. So, wait: Somebody *else* is going to have the answer for *my* business? No.

You are setting the wrong expectation for yourself, or allowing someone else to set the wrong expectation for you, if you think the success of your business relies on anyone other than *you*. The right expectation is that *you* have the answer for that important other person.

I had to realize that the power to make my business great was mine. I had to realize that the responsibility for success rested on *my* shoulders. I needed to develop the attitude that I have a gift for *this person* or *that person* with this industry.

"I need to find that special person, a real powerhouse."

Yes, when you are lucky enough to have a powerful, motivated person in your business—a person who makes sales and inspires people who, in turn, make sales—your business is, of course, going to benefit.

And so will you. But you won't know who can become that powerful, motivated person until you introduce prospects to your business and watch them learn and *grow into* that powerful, motivated person. In fact, *your prospects won't know if they are that person until they become that person.*

And guess who introduced that person to the business? You. Guess who inspired that person? Who trained your prospects and assisted them to create goals, who was a role model for them and taught them to use a process they could reliably duplicate, over and over again?

You. You are that special person.

"I need to be a better sales person."

Maybe. But it depends on what your idea of a good sales person *is.* Fake doesn't work. Showing up as authentic and professional in this business *does.*

These days, the most important discriminator in business is *authenticity.*

Bottom line: You are building relationships. Another term for this business is *relationship marketing.* What that means is that you are sharing a product or service by way of a *relationship.* You are sharing a business through *relationship.* And most relationships don't last without authenticity. People who are successful in this business share their most authentic selves, as they share the product, the service, the business, the opportunity, to as many people, often one person at a time, as many times as it takes, to achieve success for them all.

Building teams relies on you showing you care while you build community *together.*

Successful teams, working together, can build a *dynasty.*

"You can have a business in the same way that you have a hobby."

At the end of the day, network marketing is a *business.* If you treat it like a business, it will pay you like a business. If you treat it like a hobby, it will pay you like a hobby.

At the end of the day, network marketing is a business. If you treat it like a business, it will pay you like a business. If you treat it like a hobby, it will pay you like a hobby.

Are you ready to make a decision? Are you ready to have a *business?* One that has the potential to reward you greatly? Are you ready to *own* that business?

Then make the decision. Own your *business.*

"Bring people together."

Sure. You want to encourage camaraderie and cohesion in your team so, yes, you will want to "bring people together." But you will want to "bring people together" for training or calling parties where you all make time to call your contacts. Sometimes too many people on a network marketing team are actually showing up for social reasons. Consistently showing up to team meetings is great, but team members also need to be working and building their businesses and making money.

Recognition is a way to validate the efforts of those who are treating the business as a *business,* and to distinguish them from those who seem to just hang on. When you are working the business, recognition means a lot. Recognition is a big deal in network marketing, so pay attention to how your organization awards pin levels or compensation levels.

Not All Compensation Plans are Alike

Not all compensation plans (comp plans) are the same, but most award pin levels according to sales volume, as well as team building.

If your sponsor put *you* in, she or he must be doing something right. Ask "How did your sponsor do that?" When you find out, duplicate it.

If you cannot duplicate the method your sponsor

used, you might want to learn from someone else.

It is the ability to duplicate the method your sponsor used—and therefore, the method you will teach to those you sponsor—that makes this business so powerful.

"The speed of the team is the speed of the leader."

Regarding what your sponsor is teaching, and how your sponsor is teaching it, does he or she seem to be on the same page as other leaders in the business? Are other leaders on the same page as your leader? Do team leaders teach a system that can be duplicated? Do they teach a system that can be easily taught and easily followed by new team members?

In network marketing, there is no reason to reinvent the wheel. Learn what you can from your team leader, duplicate it to the letter, and as your success grows, teach it to those you bring into the business exactly how you were taught.

You don't need to reinvent the wheel.

"All you have to do is this one thing, that one thing, or this other thing."

First, using the phrase, "all you have to do ..." indicates that the speaker is already oversimplifying a process that deserves the listener's attention.

Second, while these processes, to work, must be

at least somewhat simple, they cannot be reduced in a way that detracts from their value or their effectiveness. They must be given the serious attention that they deserve—the serious attention and focus that will create success for you and your team member.

Third, when you build a team, you are responsible for that team. The more success you have, the more responsibility you have. This is why duplication is so important. If you have a duplicable system and process, you lighten your burden and the burdens of those above you and below you through the power of systems and duplication. In other words, you set up your team members for success the first time. No one is having to go back and correct your mistakes training the people you sponsored.

People use enough excuses already. You don't need to give them more excuses by teaching them in ways that can't be easily taught to the people they sponsor or by setting them up with the wrong expectations.

"A couple of hours a week is all you need to build a business."

Well, if you know exactly what to do and you know how to do it, you might be able to make this be true. But, for most people, this is not a realistic expectation.

Later in the book, you'll go through an exercise called the Tommy T, and you'll learn exactly the time commitment you need to make to get the benefits you desire.

"Everybody can do it. No one will be left behind."

This isn't true. Not everybody can do it. Only those people who are teachable and coachable, and who can learn what to do and how to do it, are going to be able to make it. And teachable is being able to learn; coachable is being able to implement what you learn in the field.

"If you build one side, I can build the other."

This statement applies to a binary business. And, fortunately, only some people will make this statement. They might make another statement, like, "I'll give you the top position in a leg." Both of these statements are indicators of unfair and unethical practices. And though I've made a few of these mistakes myself, I do not place anyone unfairly now. I do not make those statements or any like them. My practice is this: The date you join is the date you go in. I now say, "I will give you the next best position in my business, which is the first available position."

When recruiting, some people make pie in the sky promises that come in many forms. Some people slot or ratchet new members in according to some perceived stature or leadership abilities, placing them above other people who were already in the business.

This is a wrong practice. It is ethically wrong and sets wrong expectations.

Selling your business is a different story. Just as insurance agents or financial advisers can sell their book of business (their list of clients or customers), p can sell their network marketing business. Selling your business is different from slotting or ratcheting a position in a business. You might actually strive for this end goal: to sell your business. But you have to actually *have* a business that is worth a measureable amount to be able to sell it.

When a Sponsor Sets Wrong Goals or Wrong Expectations for a New Member

I believe 90 percent of people quit because they were set up with goals that were too far out in a future they were unable to imagine or goals that were too vague for them to visualize. Another reason people quit is, as I've been saying throughout this chapter, they were encouraged to have the wrong expectations.

When prospecting, we have to be very careful that we set expectations *that can actually be met*. This includes realistic goals and payouts, but it also includes any changes that you, as a sponsor, might know are planned for the company but have not yet happened.

Announcing Future Events

This is a tricky area. We need to evaluate a company regarding any announcements about future events. These announcements can be about future products, upgrades, acquisitions, software fixes, availability, or comp changes. All these are things that matter to you, your downline, and your downline's prospects.

Nothing will hurt a new person more than their expectations regarding valuable changes to their products, services, or comp plan not being met. There are some more seasoned members of your team who can deal with delays, disruption, and disappointment, but the majority of your team members cannot be expected to do so. *Prospecting* with promises of products, services, and technological capability delivered by particular dates is not a good practice. Prospecting must be based on actual facts or potentials that are clearly defined as potentials. Learning to promote what the company has *now* while casting a future vision—without making promises that are exaggerated or pegged on dates that cannot be guaranteed—is the best practice.

"Money will keep coming even if you build for a short time."

Plain and simple, this is a lie. Network marketing doesn't work that way. The only way this statement can be true is if you build strong leaders who themselves build strong businesses.

It's a good idea to imagine what would happen to your business if you stepped out—if you took a break. Would your team members be sufficiently motivated to keep going? Maybe, but maybe not.

If you build a strong business, it's *your* business. Stay with it.

The Down-Low for Your Downline

Network marketing works when we have leaders who do the heavy lifting. What is the heavy lifting? The heavy lifting of network marketing is third-party phone calls, presentations, training calls, webinars, and laying the foundation and a road map for how to proceed that is honest, ethical, and able to be duplicated.

We'll learn more about all these tools in *Chapter 4: The Tools to Succeed in Network Marketing*.

But before we get there, and now that we know many of the wrong expectations, we're going to learn about the right expectations.

People can hate this industry because they have heard these lies. What I want for you and for me is that we lead with integrity. We avoid these lies and wrong expectations and learn how to set the *right* expectations. Doing so will change this industry, and for those of us involved in this industry, we can change our world.

Chapter 2

Set the *Right* Expectations

IN CHAPTER 1, we learned some of the ways the wrong expectations can be set when we are initially introduced to an opportunity. Now, let's set the right expectations. We'll begin by setting some goals that are obtainable: Let's create a livable income and, over time, we'll go for that six- and seven-figure income you might be dreaming of, or whatever your dream might be.

The Very First Expectation

Welcome to the team! You are now an entrepreneur. And you need to have an idea of *what it takes* to be an entrepreneur. You have to understand *self*-motivation, because there is no boss standing over your shoulder. *You* are the boss.

You are the boss.

Have you heard the idea that you will be about as successful as the five most successful people in your life? If you want to make the kind of money that successful people make in the business of network marketing, you need to hang out with the most successful people in *that* business. Let's get even more specific: You need to hang out with the people who are *actually* experiencing success rather than those who are just *talking* about it.

You've already learned one way to distinguish network marketing that is not the right fit for you: by noticing if someone attempting to sell you on the business—someone who wants to sponsor you—sets any of the wrong expectations we went over in chapter 1.

Now you are going to learn how to choose the right network marketing company—a network marketing company that will serve *you*—because *you* are going to be serving *you,* and your family and friends, and the team you are going to build.

SET THE RIGHT EXPECTATIONS WITH THE TOMMY T

Would you like to get clear about exactly what it will take to make a livable income? Have you ever heard of a cost-benefit analysis (CBA)? I do what I call the Tommy T. It is the CBA I use to allow you, if I am going to sponsor you, to know exactly what it will take for you to make a livable income.

Where Do We Start?

You're going to get a single piece of paper and, using a pen, pencil, or marker, make a horizontal line a few inches from the top of the page. Next, from that horizontal line, draw a line vertically down the middle of the page to the bottom of the page. Your page should look like this:

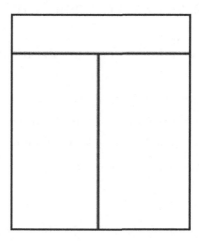

If I'm doing this with you, I'm going to print "The Tommy T," on the top. Your page will then look like this:

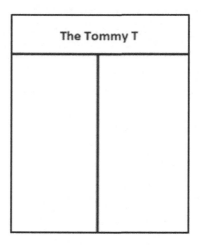

Now you are going to add the word, "Cost" at the top of the left side and "Benefit" at the top of the right.

Then divide the column on the right side of the page horizontally into two halves:

The Tommy T	
Cost	Benefit
	Top half
	Bottom half

Filling in the Tommy T

Before you fill in the Tommy T, you must be clear about two things:

- What are three tangible benefits you want to receive from the product or service the network marketing company is planning to provide?

- What is a realistic amount of money you want to earn by *one year from now* from whatever you put your time and energy into?

Let's pause here. Most network marketing companies have designed their offer and their compensation plan to provide members with a payout of anywhere from $50,000 to $80,000 in the first year *if members apply themselves diligently.*

What does "apply themselves diligently" look like? We'll get to that shortly when we go over the "cost" part of the cost-benefit analysis.

Now you're ready to fill in the Tommy T. You are going to put three tangible benefits you believe you can and want to receive from the opportunity you are considering. You are going to list those three benefits in the top half of the right side of the page.

Three Tangible Benefits

Let's look at a couple of examples of three tangible benefits so you can know what to put in this section.

We'll use the example of a technology product. This technology allows you to receive an initial amount of cryptocurrency (Bitcoin is a cryptocurrency), store that amount, and access some of it to buy items on an alternative marketplace platform.

Example One: a Technology Product

Three tangible benefits from this product and making it available to others:

- the opportunity to learn how to use and benefit from leading-edge technology in the world of cryptocurrency

- freedom from physical, traditional banking

- the opportunity to make money on a cryptocurrency that might be rapidly accruing value

Example Two: Health and Wellness Products

Now, we'll use another example: a line of health and wellness products that you will buy for yourself and present the opportunity to others to purchase and sell. Three tangible benefits from this business:

- get off blood pressure meds by losing twenty pounds

- provide your friends and family with products they really want and need

- make extra income

You will write your three, tangible benefits into the top half of the right side of the page.

A Realistic Financial Goal—One That Is Coming from Your Heart

OK, right here, we're going to get down to something that matters. In order to be motivated—in order to add a new time commitment to your life—you are going to have to focus on a goal that matters, to you, your family, or your community. In fact, this goal is your "why"—why you are spending time learning a new business, why you are connecting with others to share that business, and why you want to succeed at this business. As we say in this business, **your why should make you cry, or it isn't big enough**.

Your *why* is important. It has to come before the *what* and the *how.* You need to know your why, because, again, it is going to be your motivation. It is going to be your driver.

Your *why* is an amount of money you want to earn by *one year from now* working on a business you care about. In addition, you are going to have a few heartfelt goals you can achieve with that realistic, imaginable, amount of money.

A Few Examples

Let's try $50,000. And with that $50,000, let's imagine that you will:

- pay off debt

- travel

- create a college fund for your child

Let's try another imaginable amount, $80,000, and another set of three realistic goals:

- new kitchen appliances and a new countertop

- down payment on a new car

- the rowing machine you've been wanting

Fill in the Bottom Half of the Page

Now write the amount of money and the three benefits you can imagine you will receive from that amount of money in the bottom half of the right side of the page for the network marketing product or service *you* are consider.

What Goes on the Left Side of the Page of the Tommy T?

Now you are going to list the costs of this business opportunity in the left column.

1. Fill in the initial cost of the product or service.

2. Fill in the amount of time you will be spending to learn how to present this product; make sales; and attend any trainings, presentations, or community events.

3. If you made your first $10,000, would you commit to seeing the bigger picture by going to a national convention? Fill in the cost of any convention the company might present. (During an unusual situation like a pandemic or other travel disruption, this might be the cost of time and whatever you need to attend a Zoom meeting.)

Example One: a Technology Product

An example might be our technology product, cryptocurrency, and a platform to receive, save, and use your cryptocurrency:

Cost: $599, plus a one-time registration fee of $49.

Time commitment: ten to fifteen minutes, two or three times per day; three to four presentations or trainings per month

Bigger vision: attending a Zoom convention or using some of that first $10,000 earned to travel to a convention

Example Two: Health and Wellness Products

Our second example is the health and wellness products we considered earlier, including a starter package:

Cost: $199 for a starter package that includes supplements, meal substitutes, a meal plan, and information about health and wellness

Time commitment: ten to fifteen minutes, two to three times per day; one or two trainings (you receive) per week, and one to two business prospecting presentations (you give) per week

Bigger vision: attending a Zoom convention or using some of that first $10,000 earned to travel to an in-person convention

The Network Marketing Company You Are Considering

Now fill in the Tommy T with the information for the product or service *you* are considering.

Fill in the left side of the page with what your sponsor says will be required of you as far as money and time. If your sponsor tells you that the cost and time commitment is wildly different from these examples, you will want to find out what makes the difference. If that difference makes sense to you, you can go forward with the opportunity. If the difference doesn't seem to make sense to you, wait until an opportunity comes along that *does* make sense.

What to Look for in a Network Marketing Company

You are probably going to make your choice of a network marketing company based on one of these four things:

- the credibility and level of success of the person presenting the idea to you

- the credibility and the ethics of the founding members of the company

- the quality and uniqueness of the product or service

- the strength of the business and power of the compensation program

Your Sponsor

Every one of the companies I've been involved with came to my attention through a person in my life who I thought highly of. Remember Erik Bakewell, the person our dad called, "our family's angel"? My family thought highly of him and his wife *before* he introduced my brother and then me to the business he was excited about. Once that business had made me and Laura six figures, we *really* thought highly of him!

That special person who introduces you to your means of providing for yourself and your family may well be key to your decision to join an organization. He or she may be someone you respect, and who you are not only willing to follow into a business venture but you are honored to be associated with.

The People above Your Sponsor

OK, so maybe you are lucky enough to be the first in line after a founding member of a company. I haven't quite had that privilege. But no matter how close or how far I have been from those founding members, their morals and ethics, professionalism, genuineness, generosity, and ability to inspire have made a big impression on me. Those qualities kept me going if there were tough times. Those qualities also gave me something to aim for in my own personal and professional life.

You are going to want to learn what you can about the founding members of your company. Their actions are going to make an impact on you and your team. You are going to want to be proud to be part of *their* team.

The Product or Service

This goes without saying, right? You will want to love the product or service, and love it enough to share it. Period.

The Strength and Power of the Company

You're not in this for the money.

Wait, what? Of course you are! You are involved in a network marketing company to provide for yourself and your family. It's a business. You are here because traditional business either hasn't cut it for you or never appealed to you in the first place. There could be all kinds of reasons for this, including a past, like mine, that makes a place in corporate America or having a job a less likely alternative for you.

You will want to learn all you can about the company and the compensation plan. Once you have evaluated both, you are going to want to ask one question: Has the company done everything it has always promised it would do? If the answer is yes, you're in!

Right Expectations = You Are Ready to Go!

With an understanding of the right expectations, what do you look for in a network marketing company? More to the point, you are going to learn a lot about the company from the way the person introducing it to you behaves. When that person sets the right expectations, and doesn't spend time on the wrong ones, you will be good to go.

CHAPTER 3

THE STEPS TO SUCCESS IN NETWORK MARKETING

SO FAR, YOU HAVE LEARNED what the wrong expectations are and how to spot a company you do not want to become involved in. You've learned what the right expectations are, and you know what your *why* is. Now we are going to learn the steps to achieve success in network marketing.

STARTING THE CONVERSATION

How to Pitch Your Business

You need to learn how to *pitch* rather than how to make a sale. You are creating a possibility for someone to *get something they want.* You might think of them waiting: waiting for an opportunity, waiting for a place to put their effort, waiting for a reason to be motivated, waiting for a problem to be solved. You are showing them a system they can use to do all of these things—and reach their goals.

This is not the time for you to tell them all about you, your achievements, credentials, net worth, or whatever. This is the time for you to showcase the system and the product or service you are excited about.

Go for "No"

Of course you want to hear "yes" when you pitch your business. But, think about it. If you decide you want to rack up a certain number of no's, you won't quit prematurely at your first yes. And you won't be discouraged by any number of no's.

If I go for twenty no's in a day, I might get seven yes's. And I won't become discouraged by the no's I do get because, well, that's what I was going for!

> *"You can achieve virtually anything you want—if you're willing to hear 'no' often enough," says Andrea Waltz, co-author of Go for No!*

To learn more about how to go for no, get the book, *Go For No!,* by Andrea Waltz and Richard Fenton.

Your Sphere of Influence (SOI)

Whom do you invite to learn about your business? You want to invite members of your sphere of influence (SOI). That sphere can be described as three concentric circles.

The first circle is the inner circle. These contacts are:

- your family members

- close friends

- people you communicate with on a regular basis, who have your name in their cell phone or vice versa

- people you regularly connect with on social media

- people who come to you for advice or whom you go to for advice

These are the people you are going to be sure to invite to your business. These are the people you want to benefit from the advantages you are benefiting from. These are the people you care about enough that you sincerely want them to prosper.

The second circle is your middle circle. These contacts are:

- people you know but are not close to

- people you communicate with via cell phone or email occasionally

- people you may not contact often

- previous coworkers or friends from school or from jobs you held in the past

- people you occasionally connect with via social media

The third circle is your outer circle. These contacts are:

- people you see occasionally and may not know their name

- store owners, managers, or employees you might regularly greet

- people from the past: school, jobs, or towns

- people you're not in touch with via social media

Pitch to First-Degree Contacts:

Ask them what they know about your subject matter, whether it is financial, fitness, or health and wellness.

Or ask them any of these questions:

- Do you ever look at ways to make extra money?

- Do you like to keep your financial options open?

- If I could show you a way to make a few hundred dollars a week extra part-time, would you be interested?

- What are you doing with your discretionary

income each month?

- Are you getting good returns on your money right now? (Probably not, right?)

- Have you ever done a home-based business?

- I've always thought you would be a great business partner. Would you be interested in going into business with me?

- Do you ever look at other ways to make money, if doing so doesn't take away from what you are already doing?

Another approach is to compliment them on their work ethic, character, integrity, professionalism, drive, attitude, determination, or another positive quality. For example, "I have always admired and respected your work ethic [or other quality] when we worked together. I am working with some folks now who remind me of you. In fact, I am putting together a team and would love to have you consider being part of it. Do you have three minutes right now that I could share with you?"

Pitch to Second- and Third-Degree Contacts

These are the people you don't know really well. But they are people you can find ways to relate to. You might consider acknowledging them relative to the situations you share with them. For instance:

"You know, every time I am in here, I have the thought that you have the [nicest smile, best attitude, friendliest way about you, etc.]. I appreciate that. In fact, people with your attitude make a lot of money in my business. Would you have a few minutes to talk about my business?"

The Elephant in the Room

When prospecting, you are going to talk to people who are in your sphere. Because you know them well, you are going to know the objection they will have to spending a few minutes with you. This objection is the elephant in the room.

So lead with the elephant in the room—face the elephant in the room. When you ask to have a few minutes of their time to present your business, lead with that objection. For example, say, "Josh, I know you are busy. You've been working really hard lately. But I really think you're going to like what I have to show you."

Or, "I know you just started a new job, but I also know that you are going to want to hear what I have to tell you."

Because you addressed it first, you can eliminate it as an objection your prospect can use. Prospects will sound discourteous if they do use it, and most of the people we are even somewhat close to are not going to want to appear discourteous.

For a group presentation you might say, "I know you guys are all busy people, so I'll make this short."

Always Be Closing (ABC)

Throughout any time you are talking with your contacts, you want to be on the alert for your contact's level of interest to rise. If prospects say they are excited about something, that's the time to close the deal. Closing is about time. It is about always expecting that person to go into business with you. It's an expectation more than anything else. You can sell yourself into a sale, and then, because of overselling, you can sell yourself right out of a sale.

Assume the Sale

I don't even get in front of someone with an opportunity unless I *assume* I am going to close the sale.

Creating Connection

You are creating connection for a variety of possibilities, rather than a single possibility or a single transaction. This is where a lot of people get lost.

They take a "yes" to the sale of a product or service as a success without seeing the bigger picture. The bigger picture is the *relationship.* This is the moment to create a long-term business relationship that can and should enrich you both. In this business, consistently working on and building relationships is the key to success.

You Are the Boss

The beautiful thing about network marketing is that you can start and stop and start again whenever you want. The downside is that you can start and stop and not start again. But the up side is that you can take a month off and start again, renewed. Because you are the boss!

Believe in Yourself, and Believe in This Industry

Believe in yourself because you have something powerful to share. Once again, network marketing brings some of the most valuable products and services I've ever seen to me and to the people I love.

Believe in this industry, because it has made more millionaires than any other industry in the world. It's made more people financially fit than any other industry in the world.

BECOME A PROFESSIONAL INVITER

Professional inviters are *excited.* Professional inviters are *generous.* Professional inviters think of themselves as having a financial advantage that is so beneficial and exciting, and has such a strong potential for success, that they simply *must* invite people to learn about it.

Professional inviters are also professional promoters and professional appointment setters. Professional promoters believe in their product or service and are passionate about using this product or service to create possibilities for themselves and the people they come into contact with. Professional promoters are always contacting the people in their world. Professional promoters are always ready to schedule appointments to share their latest opportunity.

If you can master the art of simply inviting others to look at your business, you can achieve success.

The Steps to Inviting

Here are a few steps to becoming a professional inviter:

- Identify members of your sphere of influence. You might make a list, and be sure to stay in contact with them.

- When you invite members of your sphere to see your business, keep your invitation short and simple. Don't say too much!

- Maintain the correct mindset. You are here to help others achieve their financial, fitness, or health goals, and what you have to share is the most exciting way you know right now to do so.

- Embrace your responsibility. Their success depends on *you!*

- You are inviting others to learn from the person or digital resource (slide presentation, video, recorded call, text message, website) you learned from. You don't have to be the expert!

- Let the people you are inviting decide. They are the only ones who can decide if they are going to accept or reject success.

- Remember: If you don't share this with them, *someone else will.*

The Call

The call is important! This is a call you arrange with your prospect. Arrange it for the purpose of a business conversation, not as part of another casual or social call.

What to Say

Try saying this; it has worked for me! "Hey Seth [or whomever], let me ask you a simple question. Do you have three minutes to share with me right now?"

What if they say "no"? They get to say whatever they want or need to say. Your job is to ask again. Say, "OK. Well, let me know when you have a few minutes. It's really important."

If they say "yes," say, "Great! I've got something really important to share with you."

What to Do

At this point, you will bring an expert onto the call through three-way calling, or queue up a video or slide presentation, or text them a link. Of course, if you are on a three-way call, you are going to stay on the call. If you have a digital resource to share, say that you will stay on while they listen, watch, go to a website, or experience your presentation.

This call or meeting is an *introduction* to your business. Again, it must be short and simple. Once you have made your initial presentation, that three-way call with an expert or digital resource, ask your prospect if she or he wants any additional information. If so, direct your prospect to that information. If not, it may be time to close the sale.

Now the ball is in the prospect's court.

Handling "No"

If your prospect tells you no, move on. Let this particular conversation go. Maintain the relationship. Whatever you do, don't act like it has damaged your relationship in any way, because, if you are the professional I think you are, it hasn't. Because *you* know there will be other opportunities. And your relationship is, in the long run, more important than this single "no."

And, really, that "no" may mean "not yet." Or, "not this time." That "no" could easily *not* be the end of the line.

As I've heard it said, "Some will, some won't, so what? Stop whining, start working, someone's waiting—*start winning*!"

Feel, Felt, Found

Another way to handle an objection is to say, "I know how you *feel*. I *felt* that way at one time, too. But I *found* that ..." Insert your own truth at the end of the sentence.

What Is an Objection?

An objection just means that the person you are presenting to needs more information. An objection *does not* need to ruin your attitude, your day, or your motivation. Most people have learned how to say "no" to anything that seems unconventional, such as network marketing. In fact, UCLA researchers conducted a study on the number of times the average one-year-old child hears the word "no." The researchers discovered that it was four hundred times per day!

The Six Top Objections Are:

- no time

- no interest

- no money

- no sales

- no success

- pyramid

Validate these objections, because, of course, you understand them! You probably know plenty about them. Say, "thank you for bringing that up," or "thanks for being honest," or "that is exactly why you need to look at this!"

No Time

Regarding a lack of time, you can say, "Do you have three minutes a day? Can you call three people and ask them if they will get on the phone with me? If so, you can do this business. Because all you have to do is get me on the phone with them, and I'll take it from there."

Positioning

Positioning is really about where your business starts. When you are excited and motivated about the company you've joined, when you have a position within a company you feel good about, you know you are going to create a very strong team. I have over twenty years in this business. That means I have more than twenty years' experience building teams.

When I build a team, and I place someone in my downline, I very occasionally might drop someone under them, helping them create *their own* downline. Very occasionally, your upline might drop people under *you* as an extra blessing in your business build. This means you create income more quickly. This would be considered overflow, which is a gift to actually build your downline.

No Promises, No Guarantees

Please don't consider positioning a promise or a guarantee. Because, truthfully, positioning can be used to entice people and, therefore, is a wrong expectation. In most team-building situations, though, when you are blessed to be with an excited, motivated leader, positioning of this type can be a blessing.

Ultimately, however, your downline is up to *you.* The responsibility falls on *you,* as the business owner. In other words, your position in my business can help you achieve your financial goals more quickly. As you work harder building your team, the position you give new members will also benefit them.

When I get excited, I run forward with a great deal of enthusiasm. If you are lucky enough to get into *my* business, you are going to benefit from that excitement. Make this a possibility for the team, the downline, *you* build.

More about Positioning

Here are a few things I've learned over the years:

If the prospect is interested in only trying the product, *don't* be afraid to share with them the wholesale value they are receiving, as well as the value of locking a spot in your business.

If the prospect is interested in the business, and you are the expert on the three-way call, make sure to talk up the person sponsoring the prospect. Let the prospect know that, with this sponsor, he or she will be well-placed in the business and will be getting the right training and guidance to ensure success.

Make sure the prospect understands the value of the company. Let the prospect know any facts you have about what sales have looked like so far, as well as what that person's *future* can look like. You are selling the person *and* the company!!

DO I REALLY NEED TO PITCH TO MY FRIENDS?

If you don't tell your friends, someone else is going to. Think about it: If your friend knew of an amazing opportunity and *didn't* tell you about it, how would you feel?

When we procrastinate on telling our friends about our business and go to a meeting and see our friend in somebody else's business, we feel like going to what I call "the puking corner." Seeing somebody I care about in somebody else's business makes me want to puke!

For me, at the very least, I want my friends and family to know what I am doing. I figure they are a good place to get some "no's." But, of course, I wouldn't go into the conversation without actually thinking I'm going to get a "yes"!

Let Your Friends and Family Members Answer for Themselves

I remember going to an old friend with information about a business I had been in for quite a few months. He reacted to my presentation by getting angry. He said, "Why didn't you show me this months ago?"

He then jumped into my business with both feet. I was reminded that it's not my job to judge an opportunity from my friend's or family member's perspective, making up what I think their reaction is going to be. I need to give *them* the chance to give me their perspective.

If I love my product, and I'm not willing to go to my friends and family members, I probably don't believe in my product enough. If I'm not willing to tell my best friend or my mom or my daughter about something good in my life, then I must not believe in it enough.

YOU'VE GOT THEM INTERESTED. NOW WHAT? THE VALUE OF THE THIRD PARTY

So you found a product or service you love and a business, a company, an upline, you love even more. You've made initial contact, and your prospect is interested. Now what?

Now it's time to turn to a third party to provide you with the credibility you need.

Wait. You say you don't need credibility? You know everything about the product or service, and you understand the company and all the systems? You don't need someone to come in and assist you?

A System That Can Be Duplicated

You do. I promise you. Because you are going to have new members of the team, people who are new to this product, service, company, or system, and you are going to want them to duplicate the way *you* introduced *them* to the company.

You want to bring in a third party so when your new team members have someone in front of them or on the phone, they bring you in! And so the people who join their team also bring them in, or bring you in, or bring in other more experienced team members, to duplicate the method of introducing the company.

Do you get it? The third party on a phone call, in a meeting, or on social media is the key to duplicating the system.

THE KEY TO SUCCESS

Unfortunately, the step that is key to success, in my experience, is one most people fail to emphasize, or fail to emphasize enough. Do you know what it is? I'll give you a few hints:

This step loses more business than any other

step—even the steps you might focus on the most.

This step is the one most of us really, *really* don't want to think matters. (Good luck with that belief!)

Even if we get over our fear of making that initial contact, and we learn to make lots and lots of initial contacts, we may fall prey to the notion that this step makes us seem pushy. Nothing could be further from the truth.

Now, do you know what that step is? It is:

Follow-Up

We've all heard one version of it or another: "Follow-up is everything!" "The fortune is in the follow-up!" "Follow-up is the key!"

At this point, do you know why? It's because the follow-up secures the business. It nails the sale!

It also supports the *relationship.* Most people don't realize how important this step is. Because, whether or not you make a particular sale, you are creating and supporting a relationship for *future* sales, for *future* opportunities.

Do you say, "Hello. How are you?" when you greet people you are meeting? Of course you do! Why? Because it is the respectful thing to do. Because it is courteous. Because you learned to abide by what is called "common courtesy" at the front end of a meeting. What I'm telling you is that it is also common courtesy to honor the people you meet with at the *back end* of a meeting. It is a sign of courtesy, but it is also a sign of respect and a sign of your own professionalism.

You Are Wasting Your Time

I am telling you that you waste your time—all the time—if you don't follow up. I am telling you that when you make a call or send an email or text, and you don't follow up, you are wasting your time and the time of the person you attempted to connect with.

I am telling you that when you make a presentation and you don't follow up, you are not only wasting *your* time but you are wasting the time of the person who ever bothered to listen to you in the first place.

BAMFAM

Do you want to be respected for your professionalism? When you present a business system, do you want to be taken seriously? Of course you do!

Book a meeting from a meeting: BAMFAM. You will impress the people you meet with if you do this. You are going to be honoring your client's need to have their questions answered, the need to have their concerns taken seriously, and the need to have their initial interest met with your complete attention.

Remember: More important than this particular business venture is the ongoing *relationship.* Through many business relationships over the years, I have been able to share businesses I've found with team members to create multiple streams of income, and multiple ways for team members to connect and assist *one another.* Another way to say this is that many of my relationships are mutual and reciprocal. Many of us have come across an exciting product or service, and the means to bring it to market, that they then bring to the rest of us. And we are all happy to receive that information. This has led to me and the members of my network sharing and participating in a variety of business ventures, some short-term, some long-term. Many of the companies I have gotten involved with over the years have rewarded me, and the people who have participated with me, with a lifetime of income streams.

Failing to Follow Up

A few times each month, someone approaches me about a business they are pursuing. They present it to me and then ... nothing. I hear nothing more from them. They don't follow up with me to learn how I reacted to their presentation, and they don't actually ask for my business. I'm offended! Don't they think enough of me to find out how I am feeling about what they showed me? Don't they think enough of their business to find out how I feel about what, to them at the time, was the greatest thing since sliced bread? Don't they think enough of themselves to conduct themselves like a professional?

If the answer to any of those questions is no, they no longer have my interest. And they definitely don't have my money! In fact, they won't have my interest again, either.

Last month, a friend of a friend contacted me and asked me for my time. I gladly gave it. I'm interested in promising business opportunities (and you should be, too). My time and my interest were rewarded: It was, as I suspected, a good product with a great business structure and a great way to reward participants financially! And I told this person that was my belief. But I also said I needed time to pray about whether or not I wanted to become involved. I said I needed a day.

That was months ago. I haven't heard from that person since.

This friend of a friend lost that sale. But, perhaps more important, this person lost *any* sale from me going forward. This person also lost my interest and my respect.

Fear

There are two things that interfere with follow-up, and those are a fear of rejection and a simple laxity. If you are a professional, you want to cultivate this key to success. Follow-up is a habit, and a habit that creates success.

Personally, I *expect* follow-up! Because I am a professional, and I am supposing you are a professional, I *expect* follow-up! Can you imagine this: The last person you presented a business opportunity to is actually awaiting your call? What an idea!

Follow-up can be as simple as sending a text. Thank your prospect for taking the time to experience your presentation. Show that you care, that you listened to that person, and you care about the needs she or he shared with you.

Perhaps you presented a line of supplements that reduce inflammation. In response, your prospect told you about a problem with painful or stiff knees in the morning. Text that person a thank-you, and ask if the issue with painful knees has improved.

Maybe you can offer the prospect a sample as part of your follow-up. Or maybe you can ask about a prospect's pet that hasn't been well. Whatever information your prospect shared with you in the conversation when you presented your business opportunity, refer to that information to provide continuity and connection.

A gift might also be appropriate as part of your follow-up. "Hey, Jim, I wanted to thank you for taking the time to watch the video I sent. You'll be receiving a five-dollar gift card for your local coffee shop to thank you."

Remember one of those names for network marketing I shared with you, "relationship marketing"? You are building a *relationship.*

Proper Follow-up

Proper follow-up allows me to trust you and to trust the kind of business I expect you to conduct *throughout* our relationship. Because, perhaps more important than the sale itself, is the relationship.

As part of our relationship, I trust that you will respect my time and resources. I expect that you will also respect my needs as a consumer of the product or service you are sharing with me by answering my questions.

So, that's the first element of follow-up:

Step one: If I show you the business, I will answer your questions or I will bring in a third party.

If you focus on this first step, it may get you over the hump with any fear you might be feeling about making the call. Remember, you are providing information and, usually, relief, comfort, and assurance. Read that again: You are calling this business contact to provide information that will give your contact relief, comfort, and assurance. *You are giving your prospect a gift.*

Step two: Ask for the sale.

You have to actually ask for the sale, ask for the business. This element may be the greatest source of fear. It is also the greatest source of success!

Asking for the sale, asking for the business, is the number one element of the whole process that separates a successful sale from an unsuccessful sale.

How do you do it? There are all kinds of ways to do this:

"OK. What credit card do you want me to put this on?"

"I'm ready for your credit card number."

"How did you want to pay for this?"

"How many do you want?" "What size/package were you thinking you wanted?"

Ask for the Business (AFTB)

Have you ever presented a product or service, whether it was yours or your company's or a network marketing product, and then stood there, certain that a crowd was going to mob the stage, demanding your product or service?

What happened?

Nothing, right? You may have made a great presentation, but you didn't actually ask for the business.

One of the most important aspects of sales is to actually *ask for the business* (AFTB). And, believe it or not, many of us fail to do that. We somehow expect business to simply happen.

It doesn't.

We all need to ask. Learn how to pitch a great solution to your customer's problems, and then actually ask for your customer's business.

Say things like, "I'm happy to talk with you about how *you* can benefit from this business. Please connect with me after my presentation." Or, "Please let me know how I can assist you in getting into this business." Or, "If you're anything like me, you'll probably have a ton of questions in the middle of the night. Let's plan to meet tomorrow so I can answer those questions."

When You Are Assisting New Teammates

We all need to learn to ask for the business. I know I did. When we recruit new teammates and we join them on a three-way call with their prospects or they bring their prospects to a meeting, if the teammates are brand new, we probably should step up and ask for the business *for* them. On the other hand, if teammates have been in our organization for a while, at some point it is best for them to ask for the business themselves. This is a matter of coaching. We want to support our new teammates at the beginning and, when they are ready, encourage them to ask for the business on their own.

Step three: Assist your team members in setting up their business.

You did it! You just shifted a prospect from being just another person you know to being a member of your team. For me, a team member is just one step away from being a family member. In fact, over the years, my team members have become just like family!

I will talk about assisting team members in setting up their business in the next chapter's section named Supporting Your Team.

Getting A Round To It

Ever seen A Round To It?

You might never receive, or get, A Round To It. I know I never have. I have to step up and *do it*. I imagine you do, too.

Procrastination

Follow-up is a good habit. Procrastination is a bad one. If you are reading these words, you are ready. These words are teaching words, and you are ready for this teaching.

When I began my career in network marketing, I was ready. I was ready for success but, more important, I was ready for personal growth. Because personal growth is another way to talk about creating good habits and undoing bad habits, such as procrastination.

The first network marketing business I was in provided me with lots of opportunities for personal growth. And, hungry for success, ready to move forward with my financial goals, I dove into those opportunities. When I had a chance to learn, I learned. I listened to the speakers my team leaders brought to our team. I bought the books at the back of the room, and I read as much as I could to learn what I could do to succeed.

"Now, or Next to Now!"

One of those speakers used a key phrase that made a powerful impact on my life: "now, or next to now!" You have a choice: You can build your business ... now, or next to now!

When my own bad habit of procrastination comes up, I hear that speaker's words.

What Is Procrastination?

Procrastination is simply the death of opportunity. When I sense procrastination in one of my teammates, I am sad because I know an opportunity is dying, and with it, my teammate's chance to succeed.

More importantly, procrastination is something we *allow* ourselves, until we create a key to success to replace it.

Procrastination is simply not doing something that we already decided to do. And that something is usually follow-up. Procrastination can hide behind the notion that we don't know what to do but, really, we usually *do* know what to do—follow up—and we are choosing not to do it.

Imagine putting the practice of follow-up in place. With this practice, this habit, you *automatically* check in with the person you have presented an opportunity to. You *automatically* ask if that person has questions and you *automatically* ask for that person's business.

Do Not Mistake Prioritizing for Procrastination

The first couple of times you present a product or service, you may feel like you're jumping out of an airplane. It's scary and, when it succeeds, it is exhilarating. Once you've done this a few times, you begin to realize that you are *building a business.* You are building a team. You begin to think about the positions in your downline, and who you want to reward with a position close to you, because you know that is where the action is going to be. You know you are going to be supporting the people in your business, and their success is going to be key to what will support you.

Planning who you are going to invite into your business—who will be just as excited about this opportunity as you are, who you are going to shepherd to success, and who you are likely to spend your long-term career with—is really about prioritizing.

Prioritizing is important. But it should last only as long as necessary to set your priorities. Then it's time to present the business. And then, of course, it's time to follow up and make the sale!

The Inability to Take Action Builds and Builds until We Are Stuck

Remember that procrastination is a bad habit that needs to be replaced by a good habit. Ever since I first heard it, this saying has stayed with me:

---

*Opportunities do not go away; they
just go to someone else.*

The network marketing industry is a place where I consistently see this saying in action. I wish this wasn't true, but I have delayed presenting an opportunity to someone I would have enjoyed having in my business, only to see them succeed in someone else's business, on someone else's team.

Yikes. The image of someone I would have loved to work with working with someone else is my own worst nightmare.

The antidote to that bad dream is the saying, "now, or next to now." I really hope these words have as much power for you as they have had for me.

CHAPTER 4

THE TOOLS TO SUCCEED IN NETWORK MARKETING

HERE ARE THE BEST TOOLS I KNOW of to create and grow a network marketing business.

TWO HUNDRED MARBLES

Network marketing is a numbers game. To illustrate this, get two hundred marbles and two jars:

Every time you do a full presentation, either to an individual or a group, you go all the way to the close, and you get the sale, put a marble from the full jar to the other jar. By the time you have transferred all the marbles, you will have a really good business.

EASY-PEASY

An easy-peasy system is a four- or six-step process that can easily be duplicated by anyone, whether that person is a housewife, a corporate person, a salesman or a janitor. In fact, when I was first learning the easy-peasy system that I use, I wanted it to be something my 15-year-old daughter could do.

It is important that the system is easy—thus the name "easy-peasy"—because you want *anyone* on your team to be able to use it. And then you want *anyone* your team recruits to be able to use it.

Building teams in network marketing depends on duplicating whatever it is a leader does to bring some-one into the organization. You can either say there are no stars in a network marketing organization or that *absolutely everyone is a star!*

For years, people would say to me, "Tom, I'm not a salesman like you." This always confounded me, because I actually don't believe I have to be a salesman. All I have to do is utilize a system that allows members of my team to easily expose people to the products and services my team and I are on fire about—so on fire that we want to share them with *everyone.*

There are two types of easy-peasy systems. The first is what I think of as the old system. It involves direct contact, one-on-one, between the person sharing with the person receiving.

THE DIRECT CONTACT EASY-PEASY SYSTEM

Step 1: Initial exposure—phone call, text, email, and, as I like to say, "say less to more while getting in the door."

This method is about taking your prospects to the next step. It's about you offering to do something and asking your prospects to do something in return. You say:

If I _____, will you _____?

If I [do this action], will you [do this other action]?

If I	Action	Request
If I ...	*send* you a three-to ten-minute video,	will you *watch* it?
If I ...	*share* a testimony page on Facebook,	will you *take a look*?
If I ...	*send* you an invite,	will you *join* an online meeting?

Step 2: Third-party exposure—follow up to get the prospect's questions answered with a third party.

Remember that third party, the expert you bring in on phone calls? This is a person with more experience with the product or service, or with the business, than you have. This is another person to help your prospect see the bigger picture.

Step 3: Ask for the sale.

Step 4: Help the new member repeat the same process.

The Indirect Contact Method: Easy-Peasy Using the Add-Tag Message System

People may think they can get away from the easy-peasy system by using social media, but the easy-peasy system can actually *make use* of social media. The Add-Tag-Message (ATM) System uses the same exact philosophies and concepts that the original Direct

Contact method makes use of, but using social media.

The Add-Tag-Message (ATM) system allows you to connect with many more people than simple calls, texts, and emails allow. Here's how you do it:

Step 1. Create a private Facebook group for your product, service, or business. You'll want a different Facebook group for each of those things. Add any videos, announcements, events, or testimonials to the Facebook group.

Step 2. Pin a post to the top of the private group page that promotes your product or service. You can also pin part of your story—the part that explains why you want to connect with others regarding your product or service—to the top of the page. This post, about your story, might sound something like this:

"I've had such great results with this [product or service] that I had to find a way to share it with *you!*"

Step 3. Now, make it a goal to invite people to join that Facebook group.

Step 4. When prospects have joined, tag them on the pinned post or on one of those videos, announcements, events, or testimonials you placed on the group page that you want them to see. Give them time to view the various posts in the group. Facebook will continue to remind them that they've been tagged. You won't have to do that!

Step 5. Finally, message them on Facebook

Messenger to ask them what they liked. Remember the three-way call? You can do the equivalent on Messenger by doing a group message, bringing someone into the group message who has benefited or who is your designated expert. Let that third party—your expert—answer the prospect's questions. Don't be tempted to answer their questions yourself. Remember, you also want anyone you introduce to the business to be able to succeed at this, and most of your team members won't be experts on a product or service, especially if they are new to your organization.

Step 6. Consider leaving a recorded audio message on Messenger. That allows people to feel your presence in the group and feel that your contact with *them* is more personal.

THE POWER OF INTENTION

Top producers in the network marketing industry will talk about the time they made what many of us call "the decision." That decision is the one we made to take our network marketing business "to the top."

We knew this decision wouldn't affect just us. We knew it would have a profound impact on everyone around us.

We wanted to let everyone around us know what taking our business "to the top" meant for us, for our families, for our business and our business partners, and for the futures of us all.

We especially wanted our prospects to know what was possible if they made a commitment, as we had, to ourselves and to anyone we shared this opportunity with, to share and promote this business.

Thoroughly grasping this mindset of commitment and the intention to succeed took us to a totally new level.

By sharing this mindset of commitment and the intention to succeed, we felt we could gain the vital support of our family and friends. In doing so, there would be *no* mistake as to why we were doing the things we were doing. We knew we might not gain their full support; but once they knew the full power of our commitment and intention, they would not—could not—stand in our way.

This concept of "to the top" is why Laura and I named our company, "Top of the Mountain LLC." We were going to the top or be found dead on the side.

As I shared this commitment and my powerful intention, a wonderful thing happened: Many joined me for the journey. But before that happened, I had to set some boundaries.

First, I had to sit down with my parents and let them know that if I heard one more negative word about the industry, even in a joking way, our conversations were over. You see, my dad, "Daddy Dubois," used to joke around and ask, "How's that 'pyramid thing' you're in?" He'd get a big laugh out of it. Dad became a business producer, and both Mom and Dad were our biggest network marketing fans before they passed away.

Second, we needed to let our business partners in the industry know our intentions. We needed them to know that, with the Dubois family, they were standing on solid ground. We were never going to stop sharing and blessing other families' lives with network marketing. We wanted them to know we absolutely knew network marketing is the journey we were taking, and they could count on us. We were and are living by the idea that, instead of working hard for thirty to forty years and doing what we want for three to five years, we will work very hard within the industry for five years and do what we want for the rest of our lives.

We believe we can make a temporary sacrifice in exchange for a lifetime of convenience. We wanted them to know without a doubt that we loved them and we were serious about our commitment to our team and to the industry.

Third, and most important, we are never shy about strongly letting our goals be known at each and every webinar and appearance for the industry. I am telling you, when you commit to your intentions for your goals to be met, everyone will feel it from you and will want to join you. Throughout a webinar, at every chance I get, I make statements like these:

- "We are never going to stop blessing lives with network marketing."

- "We are getting all this industry has to offer, and we want you on the ride with us."

- "The sky is the limit with network marketing."

- "Network marketing is becoming a billion-dollar-a-year industry, with or without *us.*"

- "My brother has succeeded, and I have succeeded, and we can help *you* succeed."

Most of all, I like to let them know in multiple ways, please do not let your decision be a regret. We have to put our intentions in our heads, in our hearts, and out of our mouths, and I promise the results will follow!

This has been an incredible journey for me and for my wife, Laura, and for those we have blessed by sharing our network marketing businesses all along the way. Laura and I hope you can be blessed, too, by this journey of personal growth, self-discovery, and the power of intention.

TOUGH TIMES

As I write this book, we are all experiencing the tough times caused by a pandemic. At least that's what is happening right now. But there are all manner of tough times and unknown circumstances that can visit us as we go through this life of ours. Network marketing, and the principles it teaches us, allows us to connect with our family and friends, and improve our lives and the lives of those we love. Network marketing provides us with skills to improve our mindset, to succeed despite sometimes steep odds, to lighten each other's burdens, and to provide people with products and services and a sustainable business that we know can make a difference in their lives.

I believe that God has given us the opportunity to create community, and to discover how to serve one another, through the teams we build in this relationship marketing business. We can choose to be dynamic in the community by looking for ways to help, comfort, and uplift one another with the blessing of financial abundance that network marketing can bring. We can make sure we can do whatever it takes throughout the entirety of our lives!

AFFIRMATIONS

Affirmations are carefully worded statements that use the power of suggestion to affirm a positive quality that is either currently true or that the person using these statements hopes will become true. In my case, these statements reflect either the most positive view possible of what I am currently experiencing, or they reflect a future condition that I want to experience. An example of the former that is currently true is, "I make powerful and enjoyable business relationships, and many of my business contacts are now my friends." But if I were just starting out, I might use that affirmation because I want it to be true.

The idea is that our consciousness is very malleable. We can suggest something to ourselves or to others, and our minds may well believe the idea to be true, even if there is not a lot of evidence in front of us. For instance, I might go into a meeting looking well-dressed and confident, and convince you that I am successful—and I might have just started my business that very day! (I probably did that a few times!)

Confidence

Of course, our confidence in ourselves, and in our product or service or our business, is really what we want to convey to those we meet. Another way to say this is that we are selling what has made us feel good, what has made us so confident and successful.

We repeat affirmations usually silently to ourselves, although we can also say them aloud. Through repetition, affirmations begin creating a reality in our heads that may or may not exist in our lives. This, though, is the first step to them becoming reality! In other words, if I can believe the statement, I can begin to behave in a way that will eventually make that statement true.

What Makes an Affirmation?

An affirmation has to be worded in a positive way. It is said that the subconscious mind cannot process a negative statement. Although you might want it to be true that you never fail to pay a debt, repeating, "I never fail to pay a debt" has the word "never" in it. The subconscious mind will hear the word "never" and decide that I will never be able to pay my debts! Instead, we look for a way to make the statement positive. We might use, "I always pay my debts."

But, really, we don't want to even suggest having debts to the subconscious mind. We might, instead, use "I enjoy making _____ [fill in the blank] each day/week/month/year."

And that's another thing about affirmations: You need to actually believe them. Maybe thinking about how much you make a day isn't something you can conceive of. Instead, you do better thinking about another increment, such as a week, month, or year.

Affirmations Must Be Realistic and Believable

I remember when I first started using affirmations. Those statements were very modest compared to the ones I make now! Because of the success I have experienced, I believe in myself to a greater degree now than I ever did before.

My Affirmations

- Everybody wants to be in business with me.

- Everybody wants to buy a big package.

- I am one of the top recruiters and trainers in the network marketing industry.

- I attract positive-minded people to me; I draw all things positive to myself.

- I make powerful and enjoyable business relationships, and many of my business contacts are now my friends.

- People like and trust me; they want to learn more about the benefits I offer.

- I inspire others to make their lives work to the maximum, because I have shared my opportunity with them.

- I am a giving, sharing person. I share my business knowing that I am helping others.

- I have aligned myself with a great network marketing company. My leaders care about people and strive to do what is right for them, just as I do.

Your Affirmations

Now, what are *your* affirmations? Write one strong affirmation and then at least three more. Write them out every day and post a copy where you can see them. Say them out loud every day and repeat them silently to yourself every day.

You can even see your success reflected in the affirmations you write. Maybe you start out stating a modest amount of income that you make in a period of time such as a week or month and, after a few months, you have to increase the amount to make it greater than your *current* success!

THE TENS

There are two sets of ten items that will help you take your business to the highest possible level. The first is a set of ten questions you can ask yourself. The second is a set of ten mistakes people can make when joining a network marketing company.

Answering Ten Questions

Answering these ten questions will provide you with the excitement you need to keep going. You can share these with your downline—and watch the excitement spread!

I hope you will be as inspired by them as I have been.

But before we get to them, there are three aspects of the mind that make these questions so powerful. They are:

1. **The mind can focus on only one thing at a time.** When you get really clear about what your focus is each and every day, you will let loose the greatest amount of power your mind is capable of.

2. **The mind creates in the direction of its focus.** In the same way that you can drive across the full expanse of this country, from one coast to

the other, seeing only what shows up in your headlights, you can create whatever is within your area of focus.

3. **The mind triggers on questions.** Your mind is amazingly curious. You were built to solve problems and answer questions. Questions trigger answers—or the robust search for answers.

THE TEN QUESTIONS

1. What can I do *today* to increase my productivity in the industry?

   Let your mind work, and write it down.

2. Who do I know that I need to share my business with *now*?

   Let your mind work, and write it down.

3. Who do I know that needs to make a decision in the industry now so they do not weigh down my growth? Or what closure rate of shown prospects do I need?

Let your mind work, and write it down.

4. What circumstances am I allowing to stand in the way of my business goals?

Let your mind work, and write it down.

5. How can I clear my schedule to allow my fortune to be built with network marketing?

Let your mind work, and write it down.

6. How can I watch for the people God is going to place in my path today for my business and effectively prospect them?

Let your mind work, and write it down.

7. What books, CDs, calls, and mentors should I pursue today to help me become a master of me and my business?

Let your mind work, and write it down.

8. Who can I help build their business today?

Let your mind work, and write it down.

9. Moving all excuses aside, what action can I take today to set up the greatest week I have had so far in network marketing?

Let your mind work, and write it down.

10. What are all the things I am grateful for about network marketing? This is your "gratitude list." Write it down and then post it where you can see it. Focusing on what you want is powerful. Focusing on what you are grateful for might even be more powerful!

Let your mind work and make a huge network. Your business will be everything you want it to be.

As you grow your business, you are building trust with yourself. Remember credibility? You are increasing your credibility with *yourself*!

If you ask yourself those ten questions, you will build a successful marketing business.

THE TEN BIGGEST MISTAKES PEOPLE MAKE WHEN JOINING A NETWORK MARKETING COMPANY

These are the ten biggest mistakes I've seen:

1. Believing that you will make money quickly without making the proper efforts. Believing in a "get rich quick" opportunity.

2. Quitting too soon.

    "Quitting three feet from gold," is the way I have heard this said. Don't do it!

3. Allowing a dream stealer to steal your dream.

    You know them: the people who like to shoot down your dream, remind you that your place is not to go higher, usually because they don't want you to do better than them or leave them behind.

4. Having unrealistic expectations of success.

    Remember the first chapter, "Expose the Wrong Expectations"? You might want to read about all the wrong expectations I have heard in my career in network marketing—and then read them again. You want to join a team with a leader who sets the right expectations, and then you will want to turn around and do the same.

5. Expecting others to build your business.

    I think this one speaks for itself. It's *your* business. Work it.

6. Not using systems.

   The network marketing company you have joined has systems. These systems were designed by people who used them and profited from using them. Don't try to reinvent the wheel! Use the systems. They work!

7. Trusting in things that you are told without getting proof that what you are told is true.

8. Not researching a product or company.

   Do your research!

9. Letting the wrong people in business with you just for a "yes."

   Think about it: If you imagine that the business you have joined is providing you with a career—with a lifetime of profits—then who do you want with you? Who do you want walking beside you for the rest of your earning years? Think about this with each and every person you invite into your business, even if you think they are just going to buy a single product or service and they don't seem initially interested in the business.

   This is a long-term decision. Treat it as such, and you will be pleased with the team you build.

10. And maybe the most important mistake of all: getting desperate.

    You aren't going to make good decisions from a place of desperation. No one ever has. You are in an industry that generates success stories. Treat your story like a success story, even before you are fully successful, and you will have a greater chance of *being* successful.

SUPPORTING YOUR TEAM

Promote, Promote, Promote

In the world of network marketing, we are sales people. We are also networkers. Maybe the most important thing we are, though, is cheerleaders, promoting our business to those we have already recruited, as well as to those we plan to recruit.

We have to maintain the belief that what we are selling—and remember, we are always selling the business, not just the product or service—is the solution to the problem of how to financially support ourselves and our families. We have to maintain that belief in ourselves as well as in everyone who has trusted us with their own financial future.

But more than that, network marketing is, for many of us, a path to personal growth. Remember the saying I shared with you some pages back? "Network marketing is personal growth with a paycheck." I don't know how you feel about this but, for me, network marketing opened my eyes to many positive steps that have helped me learn and grow and heal my past. I believe network marketing can be that for you, too.

Promoting the Business Is Promoting Ourselves

All the businesses I have been involved with in this industry have brought me to where I am today. And where I am today is better than I could ever have imagined! Laura and I have the life we always wanted, and we are so happy to be able to assist so many other people in having the lives they have always wanted.

I want to promote *you!* I want you to move upward in the world, continuing to increase your level of success. As you and I succeed, and as we share our businesses, we are promoting everyone in our world who chooses to join us. We are learning, and growing, and becoming more successful each day, and we have the opportunity through network marketing to make success available to others. It doesn't get much better than that!

SHARE THIS BOOK, SHARE THESE STEPS

Share the ideas, the steps, and the tools I've shared with you here, in these pages. Share this book with your downline. Heck, share it with your upline! Share this book even if someone does not choose to join you in your business. These ideas are tried and true steps to success in network marketing. Many of these steps will allow you to succeed in any endeavor—even traditional business.

And, really, many of these steps will allow you to become a more well-rounded, positive, and powerful person—an influencer and promoter in your family, among your friends, and in your community.

You just joined me on a journey of success and self-discovery. Thank you! You and I are among the percentage of people who work to improve their situation in the world—and succeed. You are my people, and I hope, after reading this book, you can feel like I'm one of yours.

Here's to Success

Laura and I wish to share our success with *you* and with those you will be sharing *your* success with. We are all part of the world of multilevel marketing—part of a family of individuals who use ambition and personal growth, desire and relationship, to create success for ourselves and many of the people we come in contact with.

Here's to *you!*

Acknowledgments

I WISH TO ACKNOWLEDGE AND THANK all of these professionals who helped me with my 1st incredible book!

Fran Gallaher is my friend, Business Coach and Ghost Writer of this book! Her business, Really Flourish LLC, Highlights Intuitive Life Coaching, Online Intuition Training, Classes, Seminars, Groups and Retreats. "Really Flourish" is a company that offers coaching, classes, seminars, groups and retreats that make extraordinary experience accessible—as a part of everyday life, a part of the workplace and a part of your evolutionary path. "Really Flourish" was founded in 1994 by Fran Gallaher to bring the benefits of coaching, meditation and intuition to individuals and businesses.

Lisa Jo Keith with Blaze Branding Solutions : Blaze Branding helps transitioning professionals with clear, connecting visual images that grow businesses from good to great!

Victoria Wolf with Wolf Design and Marketing: *Tell the World Who You Are* with award-winning book cover design, interior formatting and design and eBook formatting for self-publishing authors.

Richard Wolf: Senior Self-Publishing Consultant & Trainer, Publishing Consultant. As your project manager, Richard will guide you step-by-step through the myriad of tasks involved in self-publishing your book.

Jan Stapleton with Fearless Communications We provide clear, powerful content people will actually read; impeccable editing; flawless grammar & sentence structure; freedom from jargon, buzz words and trendy goobledygook; pain-free comprehension.

ABOUT THE AUTHOR

THOMAS DUBOIS was not a likely candidate for success: through a series of bad choices, his own and those of the adults he trusted, Thomas Dubois found what he thought was the answer to his problems: in the bottom of a bottle, at the end of a pipe or a rolled up dollar bill, and whatever else he could get his hands on. After too many years to count, he ended up homeless, walking down the streets of Houston with all he had left: his clothes in two beat-up plastic trash bags.

With a felony on his record and only a short period of sobriety under his belt, any success he could hope for seemed limited. But his brother, Bob, gave him that one more chance that made the difference: the opportunity to manage one of Bob's direct mail advertising franchises. Thomas began with one franchise, grew it to three successful franchises, and then, as his father used to say, "our family's angel" paid Bob a visit and introduced him, and he, in turn, introduced Thomas, to the world of network marketing.

20 years later, Thomas and his wife, Laura, are multiple business owners including Barking Beauties, a dog grooming shop in Aspen, Colorado, several network marketing companies he has taken to top levels, as well as forays into the world of crypto currency, all of which provide he and Laura with a seven-figure income. He has been featured twice in *Success From Home Magazine* and has sponsored thousands of others in the industry he loves.

Thomas has never forgotten the grace that brought him to sobriety and eventual recovery. As a result, he has a passion for helping others in sobriety and holds his own 12-Step meeting and supports sober living homes through Step Seven Ministries in Parker, Colorado.

Thomas and Laura live with their beautifully groomed standard poodles in Glenwood Springs, Colorado.

Made in the USA
Columbia, SC
27 March 2021